Peace of my Mind

El Evans

BookLeaf Publishing

India | USA | UK

Presentation by *BookLeaf Publishing*

Web: www.bookleafpub.com

E-mail: info@bookleafpub.com

ISBN: 9789357446020

First edition 2022

DEDICATION

To everyone who encouraged and supported me along the way.

PREFACE

Hello there! Nice to meet you, I'm El, thank you for being here!

I wrote this book to act as a reminder of the good things in life: good puns, good people, good music, and sometimes even a good cry. I wanted to convey a powerful sense of joy, and discuss things that bring me joy personally. I hope this book brings you some happiness, and that you'll like it as much as I liked writing it.

Qualia

With all the words in the world at my disposal
I still can't tell you just what it's like

To feel the music deep in your chest
Pounding in time with your heart
Pulling at your soul
Urging you to move with the beat

To taste that first sip of tea
The delicate flavours intermingled into a
symphony of flavour
Just the right temperature
Perfectly sweetened

To hear the bees in the garden
The soft buzzing as they go from flower to
flower
Each individual hum overlapping with each
other
A one-note symphony

To see that person face to face
Their smile
All those tiny details not captured through a
screen

So obvious to you now

To smell the pages of old books
The ink long dried
Almost stale from years in a library
But somehow still so fresh

I cannot describe what it's like
But it is truly
Beautiful

Gestalt

You are so much more
Than just the sum of your parts

Just as the most sonorous symphony
Is more than its individual instruments

It is passion
Sorrow
Anger
Love

It is the occasional, inevitable wrong note
Surrounded by so many beautiful layers
All coming together
To create something magical
Something greater

Something beautiful.

Memory

It is that night in Japan
Riding the train, looking out the window
And seeing all the lights illuminated
The foreign abruptly familiar

It is summer camp
The smell of bug spray, sunscreen, and coffee
The wet grass beneath your feet
Finally finding your voice during Piano Man

It is exams
The room a little too cold
Desks arranged a little too neatly
Floors a little too loud

It is tinged in sepia
Bright and fading simultaneously
Happy and sad
But wholly yours alone.

Cartesian theatre

Maybe I am a passive observer
Stuck in my own little movie theatre of a brain
Watching life go by
My own thoughts, the soundtrack
Each memory, a new scene

But
What an incredible story it is
So many plot twists
Ups and downs
Even the dull moments are riveting
A story unlike any other

Truly, a cinematic masterpiece

Dreams

Come, my Darling
There are far more fantastical adventures
awaiting you
You just need to close your eyes
And let your mind do the rest
The edges will be softer in the morning
Turned from broken shards
To sea glass

Dualism

I am thought and electricity
Joy and dopamine
Memories and cortices

I am the world I perceive and the mechanisms
that allow it
Mind and body
Physical and mental

I am boundless potential and physical
boundaries
Extending infinitely inward and outward limits
Infinite and constrained

I am.

Neurons

A firework activation pattern
Electricity scattered all across
Hinting at endless thoughts
Possibilities
Experiences
With just
A simple
Spark.

Behaviourism

All it takes is time
A behaviour
A prompt
And intentional or not, it happens
Worms its way into your life
And becomes a response

It's why my heart rushes
Every time I see your name
Pop up on my silly little screen

Logic

In order for something to be logically sound
It must have all true statements
And a true conclusion

How can it be, then
That even with all of the true statements
presented
(You like me as a person)
*(You think it's cute when I go on long-winded
rants about the mind)*
*(You see my flaws and don't care that I'm a little
messed up)*
I still find it completely nonsensical
The sound conclusion we ended up at
(I get to call you mine)

Reductionism

Everything can be simplified
Slowly broken into smaller and smaller bits
Until all that remains is the basics of the
universe

Sitting on the bus, holding your hand, laughing
with you
The memory of your hand in mine
The nice, fuzzy feelings it brings up
A repeated neuron firing pattern resulting in an
oxytocin release
Sodium gates opening in response to a stimulus
to allow for an action potential
Singular sodium ions
Protons, neutrons, electrons
Quarks
Magic

The mind

You are lightning and diamond
Powered by rivers and earth
Conscious by some miracle of the universe

You are a masterpiece of coincidences
Utterly unknowable unlikelihoods
And forces that we may never truly solve

Revel in your creation.

Entropy

Here I stand
Arms open
Utterly joyful in my own chaos
Laughing through the storm
I embrace the unknown

Hurt

My Darling,
You don't have to be okay all the time
You are allowed to be hurting
You are allowed to seek comfort
You are allowed to let others see when things are
bad and help you through it
There's no weakness in vulnerability

My Darling,
You deserve to be taken care of.

Sound

It's more than just sound waves
It's the blush that comes to your cheeks after
hearing something sweet
It's the bad dancing elicited by your favourite
song
It's the slowed heart rate from birds and bees
and storms
It's the wave of affection caused by their out of
tune singing
It's the joy of movement spurred on by melodies

It's sensation.

Taste

That perfect first sip of tea
Not too hot, just barely drinkable
Sweet enough to counteract the bitter
Just right

Your favourite comfort food on a hard day
Somehow tasting better because of the
challenges
Things may not be great
But they're a little better now

Your parent's cooking after a long time away
How nobody can make it quite like them
All the love that went into it
Reminding you that you are home once again

The cheap pizza bought late at night
You just need food, and it serves its purpose
But somehow it tastes so much better
Being shared with friends

Smell

The earth after rain,
The freshness of it,
A renewal of life

The flowers outside
Almost cloying
You can almost understand the appeal to bees

The ocean
Endlessly churning
The musk somehow so comforting

Memories reawakened by a breeze

Touch

It's just a connection
Something saying you're not alone
A reassurance of unity

So tell me
If it's such a tiny thing
Why does it make my heart leap into my throat
To see your fingers entwined with mine?

Sight

Looking up to see the world
Is worth the stumbles

Seeing their smile
The sunset
The buildings speckled across the city
The massive expanse of the universe extending
endlessly outwards
It's all worth any slip-ups from the path.

Moths

I would say you give me butterflies
But that is simply not true
Though butterflies are drawn to sweet things
But no

You give me moths
Drawn to your light
Leaving my heart aflutter
Making everything fuzzy

Wanderlust

You could never explain it
The tug at your soul
The craving for freedom
The urge to just run away
To see what the world has to offer
To live boundlessly
To learn so much more than you ever thought
possible

(How lovely the headlights are at three AM)

Endings

How utterly human it is
To want to linger on the last page
Not quite ready to end the story
Not ready to let go
To take comfort in the familiar before the
memories begin to collect dust
How beautiful it is to have the memories at all
To have a final page worth lingering on
Not to be forgotten
Not to be abandoned
But to have provided some joy, somewhere in
these pages

How wonderful it was to have you come along
To join me on the final page
Sharing a moment with me
Sharing your time
I hope you enjoyed my words.